COMPUTER SENSE COMPUTER NONSENSE

COMPUTER SENSE COMPUTER NONSENSE

Seymour Simon

Illustrated by

Steven Lindblom

J.B. Lippincott   New York

Computer Sense, Computer Nonsense
Text copyright © 1984 by Seymour Simon
Illustrations copyright © 1984 by Steven W. Lindblom
All rights reserved. No part of this book may be
used or reproduced in any manner whatsoever without
written permission except in the case of brief quotations
embodied in critical articles and reviews. Printed in
the United States of America. For information address
J.B. Lippincott Junior Books, 10 East 53rd Street,
New York, N.Y. 10022. Published simultaneously in
Canada by Fitzhenry & Whiteside Limited, Toronto.
Designed by Trish Parcell
10 9 8 7 6 5 4 3 2 1
First Edition

Library of Congress Cataloging in Publication Data
Simon, Seymour.
    Computer sense, computer nonsense.

    Summary: discusses twenty-four common beliefs
about computers, such as "Computers are smarter than
people" and "Computers can smell flowers," concluding
they are either sense or nonsense.
    1. Computers—Juvenile literature. [1. Computers]
I. Lindblom, Steven, ill. II. Title.
QA76.23.S55 1984   001.64   83-49492
ISBN 0-397-32085-X
ISBN 0-397-32086-8 (lib. bdg.)

Contents

Introduction

Can computers take over the world? Are computers smarter than people? Can computers smell flowers? You have probably heard a lot about computers. It seems that almost everyone is talking about them these days. But do you know which of the things you hear make sense? Or which ones are nonsense?

In this book, we'll look at some of the things people say about computers. You'll find out which ones to believe and which not to believe. You'll also find out the reasons why a statement is true or why it is false. Even if you use computers in school or own a home computer, you may be surprised at some of the answers. As you will see, truth is sometimes stranger than fiction!

Computers Can Take
Over the World

NONSENSE

In the movie *2001: A Space Odyssey*, astronauts are on a mission to find the source of a mysterious signal in space. They travel on a ship run by the computer HAL. HAL decides that the humans aboard the ship are interfering with the mission and begins to kill them.

In the movie *War Games*, the supercomputer of the Defense Department begins to play the game Global Thermonuclear War. But the computer is playing the game for real. It's about to launch nuclear missiles at the Soviet Union, and no one knows how to stop the computer from continuing the game.

Other movies such as *The Forbin Project*, *Demon Seed*, and *Tron* feature good humans versus out-of-control computers. Are these movies realistic? Can a computer go off on its own and start a war or attack humans? Can a computer take over the world?

The answer is that a computer does only

what its program tells it to do. A computer follows its orders exactly. It cannot decide by itself what to do. So the idea of a computer taking over the world is nonsense.

That doesn't mean that computers can't be harmful to us. Computers do run the programs that direct missiles and other weapons, for example. But a human being has to create the program and order the program to be run. A computer cannot do either on its own.

Computers Are a New Invention

NONSENSE

Many people think computers have been around for just a few years. But computers date back thousands of years—the abacus, for example. The abacus is a computer in that it is a device for doing mathematical problems. About 150 years ago, a personal computer was invented by Charles Babbage, an Englishman. It was called an "Analytical Engine." It was a mechanical computer—it used gears, not electronic circuitry, but it had a memory and could be programmed.

The first electronic digital computer (that's the kind we use today) was completed in 1946 at the University of Pennsylvania. It was named **ENIAC** for the words "Electronic Numerical Integrator And Calculator." **ENIAC** filled a large room and weighed thirty tons. It was powered by over 18,000 vacuum tubes. **ENIAC** could run for only seven or eight minutes on average without a tube failing.

ENIAC was in use for ten years before it was retired.

In the 1960's vacuum tubes were replaced by smaller, more efficient transistors. Then in the early 1970's, tiny silicon chips came into use, each containing thousands of circuits. A computer as powerful as ENIAC now took up the space of a desk. As the years passed, computers grew even smaller and more powerful.

The first personal computer came on the market in 1975. It was called the Altair 8800 and was sold in the form of a kit. In a few years, many other personal computers were introduced. Nowadays, you can buy a computer that is as small as a typewriter and much more powerful than ENIAC.

Computers Are Smarter Than People

NONSENSE

Some people think computers are smarter than people because, for example, a computer can do math calculations millions of times faster. But you can recognize your friend's face among photographs of hundreds of children in your school, and no computer can do that. And you know when a joke is funny, and no computer knows that. A computer does some things very well. Other things a computer cannot do at all.

It doesn't make sense to say that a computer is smarter or dumber than a person. A computer just does things differently. In a way, a computer knows only two things: yes and no. An electric circuit is either open or closed; yes or no. All the information that is fed into a computer is translated into two symbols: 0 and 1. Every number and every letter is coded in zeros and ones. To the computer, 0 means off, 1 means on. All deci-

sions are either 0 or 1, yes or no—never maybe.

A great many yes/no or off/on circuits can fit into a small space. In a tiny space the size of your fingernail, a computer can have more than a million of these circuits. As a computer does its work, each of these circuits opens and closes thousands of times a second. But your brain has many more nerve cells than a computer has circuits. A human brain has about 100,000 million nerve cells! And they interact with each other in ways even the most powerful computer in the world cannot.

Computers Never Forget

NONSENSE

Computers have three kinds of memories. Each kind is different and has a different use. And one of the important kinds of memory is lost every time you shut off the electrical power to the computer. So to say a computer never forgets anything is nonsense.

The kind of memory that is switched on and off is called RAM. The letters stand for the words "Random Access Memory." It's a kind of temporary memory like jottings on a scratch pad or in a notebook. RAM is a read/write memory. You can *write* information into RAM using a keyboard or some other input device. You can *read* information from RAM with a TV screen or a printer. But unless you store the information in a different kind of memory in the computer, the information will be lost when the computer's power is turned off.

Another kind of memory contained in computers is called ROM. That stands for "Read

Only Memory." This contains the built-in instructions a computer needs to operate. Information can only be read from ROM, not written into it. ROMs are memory chips that are installed at the factory where the computer is made. ROM is permanent memory. It's always present in the computer and available whenever you turn on the power.

A third kind of memory is stored either on magnetic plastic or magnetic tape in the form of cassettes or disks. You can write information to this kind of memory, and unless you decide to erase the information, it will be stored permanently. A computer disk or cassette works just like a cassette you record music on. You can keep the music for as long as you want and then erase it and store some new music.

The Heart of a Computer
Is Made from Sand

SENSE

The control centers of today's modern computers are tiny silver-gray squares no bigger than your fingernail. These squares are called chips or microchips. Each chip is covered by thousands of electrical pathways or circuits. And believe it or not, the chips are made from silicon, a material found in beach sand.

The silicon in a chip has to be purified to get rid of other materials. This is done by heating sand in a tub. The silicon melts under

high heat. As the silicon melts, it floats to the top. Impurities settle to the bottom. A tiny crystal of pure silicon is then lowered into the molten silicon. The silicon cools and forms a large crystal around the pure crystal.

The large crystal is then put on a slicing machine. The machine slices the silicon into thin sections called wafers. Thousands of wafers can be made from a single silicon crystal. The wafers are put on trays and polished to a mirrorlike smoothness.

Automatic machinery is used to coat the wafers with a thin film that is sensitive to light. The electrical circuits are projected on the wafer, and the wafer is developed in a darkroom. Then acid is used to etch the circuits permanently.

The wafer is baked and washed. Wafers are handled by robot hands, never by human hands. The clean wafer is then cut up. Some wafers are cut into from one to two hundred individual chips. Each chip is sealed in a protective casing which has little wires leading in and out. It is now ready to become the heart of a computer.

Computers Are Useless
without a Program

A computer without a program is like a cassette player without a cassette: neither is of much use. Just as you use a cassette player to listen to a music cassette, you use a computer to run a program such as a video game. The main difference is that a computer program usually needs some input from the person using it.

A computer program is a numbered list of instructions that make the computer do a particular job. Computer programs can be loaded into a computer in several different ways. You can type in a program on a keyboard connected to a computer. This takes a lot of work, and you must know the special language, or languages your computer understands. Most programs are inputted into home computers from a cassette tape, a cartridge, or a disk. Computer experts say that the program is being run rather than being

played. Running a program is as easy as playing a tape or a record.

Computer programs can do lots of things. They can be used in calculating all kinds of mathematical problems. They can be used to balance a checkbook or organize a family budget. They can maintain a file system for your record or baseball card collection. They can help you draw pictures, compose music, or learn a foreign language. They can help you write a letter or a book. They can let you play all kinds of games.

Computers All Understand the Same Language

NONSENSE

A computer language is a set of words, numbers, or symbols that you can use to give a computer instructions. BASIC is the language used most often with home computers. The program on page 26 is written in BASIC. It will run on most home computers, because home computers generally understand some version of BASIC.

But there are lots of other computer languages. Many are designed to carry out special jobs. If you want your home computer to understand one of these, you will have to buy a program that will load that language into your computer's memory. The program allows the computer to understand the instructions you enter in that particular language.

Computer languages that use words and numbers and symbols that are familiar to us are called *high-level languages*. BASIC is a

high-level language. So are FORTRAN, COBOL, and LOGO. A *low-level language* is closer to the computer's own binary code. There are two main types of low-level language—machine code and assembly code. These are strings of numbers and letters that make no apparent sense—unless of course you spend time studying the languages.

Computers Are Easy to Operate

SENSE

Computers are supposed to be difficult to use. You're supposed to have to study a lot to become computer-literate. Until very recently, that was true. But computers have changed a great deal over the past few years. Today's home computers have become user-friendly— that means they are easy to use.

Most home computers can be unpacked and set up in less than an hour. You can begin working with them in as short a time as it takes you to plug in a program cartridge and read the simple instructions on the screen. Today's home computers are for anyone, not just for superbrains and computer whizzes.

In fact, there are programs today that can be used by kindergarten and even preschool children. For example, children can draw with their fingers on a special pad and see their drawing appear on the screen in front of them. Then they can add color to their drawings just by pressing certain buttons.

Nursery schools in many parts of the country are buying computers. There are programs to help prepare the children for reading and math, and to teach them colors and shapes and concepts such as "under" and "over."

Of course, to learn to write complex programs for a computer—or even to use some programs—still requires a lot of training.

Computers Are Good Only at Working with Numbers

NONSENSE

Computers are good for many different kinds of work besides mathematical calculations. For example, word processing is an important task that computers do well. In many homes and offices where there are computers, word processors have replaced typewriters just as typewriters once replaced pens.

With a word processor computer, the words you type appear first on a video screen. You can change the words, move them around, delete them, or arrange the paragraphs differently. When you are satisfied with what you have written, you use a computer-controlled printer to print out the words on paper.

Farmers, athletes, dancers, musicians, and artists can all use computers in their work. Dancers and athletes use a special device to input their motions into a computer. An outline figure of them in action appears on the computer screen. They watch the figure on the screen to learn what they are doing right and what they are doing wrong. This helps them become better at their work.

Farmers use computers to keep track of the kinds and amounts of food their animals eat. They use computers to tell them when and what kinds of fertilizers to use on their crops. Artists use computers to make sketches and to check how different colors will look before they make a final drawing or painting. Musicians use computers to compose music. Almost any worker can be helped by a computer in some way or another.

Computers Can't Hear, See, or Talk

NONSENSE

Computers can "hear" you speak and answer in words. They can "see" a scene or a face and store it in memory. All they need in order to do these things are special attachments. If you've ever played a game that has sound on it, you may have already heard a home computer talk. Some home computers even have attachments that will allow you to program them to speak the words you select. And at least one home computer has a voice recognition circuit. You can give instructions to the computer just by talking to it.

Modern department stores and supermarkets use computers to "see" things. The packaging on many items in the stores has black bars printed on it. Some of the bars are thick and some are thin. The bars are a kind of code that identifies what the item is. When the bars are passed across a special light reader near the cash register, a signal goes to a central computer. The price and description of the item are sent back and appear on the sales receipt. The computer keeps track of the changes in the store's inventory.

Of course, computers don't really hear, see, or talk in the same way people hear, see, and talk. Computers have to be programmed or instructed exactly what to say or do in every case. You can guess at the meaning of a new word that you hear for the first time. A computer will just signal that it doesn't understand.

Computers Can Smell Flowers

SENSE

Computers can be programmed to do many things—even tell the difference between roses and lilacs. Of course, computers need a special kind of "nose" to do this. The electronic "nose" samples the air and sends signals to a memory chip in the computer. The signals are compared to information stored in the memory chip. If the signals match the information for "rose," the computer identifies the smell.

Electronic sniffers will be able to do many things in industry. Imagine a sniffer in a perfume factory. It will be able to tell if a batch of perfume being produced is incorrectly mixed. "Nosy" computers may even be able to sniff out the good from the bad in products like packaged foods and beverages.

Computer noses, however, will have to become much better to match the smelling ability of a dog. A dog's sense of smell is incredible. Bloodhounds, for example, have

over 200 million nerve cells that detect odors. Specially trained bloodhounds and other kinds of dogs are used by customs officials to find illegal drugs in suitcases. It isn't even necessary to open the suitcase. One sniff at the lock is enough for the dog. The smell has come through the tiny openings in the lock. No computer nose can do that...yet.

Computers Can Help
You Do Your Homework

SENSE

Computers can help you do your homework in all kinds of ways. They can even make it easy to write the following sentence one hundred times: "I will not hit Marilyn again." All you have to do is write a simple program, run it, and print out the results.

Of course, there are better ways to use a computer to help do your homework. One way is to take home a cassette or disk containing a particular lesson and run it on your computer. The lesson can be in the form of a new learning experience, a drill, or a review. It can be an interactive lesson—that is, it can ask you questions and you then must input your answers. And you can do the lessons as many times as you want—a computer never gets bored.

All kinds of computer programs are now being used as learning tools. For example, children (and older people as well) are learn-

ing to type rapidly with programs such as Typing Tutor, Type Attack, and MasterType. You can immediately tell how well you are doing and even have fun while practicing.

The most popular use of a computer to help with homework is with a word processing program. A word processor lets you type on a keyboard and see the words on a screen in front of you. You don't have to worry about coming to the end of a line. The word processor goes to the next line automatically. You never have to retype a whole page to correct a few errors. A word processor allows you to make changes and corrections quickly and easily. It allows you to rearrange sentences, paragraphs, and even pages of material. It lets you think about what you are writing without worrying too much about neatness. Then when you like what you have written, all you do is push a key and your poem, story, or essay is printed. The words you are reading now were first written on a word processor by the author of this book.

*Here is a program written in BASIC, a language most computers understand. This program will appear on the screen. To direct the output to a printer, you would need to add additional commands.

```
NEW
10 FOR X=1 TO 100
20 PRINT "I WILL NOT HIT MARILYN AGAIN"
30 NEXT X
40 END
```

Computer Users Never
Talk to Anyone

NONSENSE

Many people think that children and adults who spend a lot of time using computers never talk to anyone human. But people all over the world are using their home computers to send messages, to talk to friends, to receive mail, to get the latest news and sports scores, to get up-to-date weather forecasts, to do research, and even to shop without ever leaving home. Computer users say that they are "on-line" with the world.

You need only three things to go on-line. First, you need a computer. The computer you use can be small and inexpensive, or as powerful and costly as a multithousand-dollar office computer. Second, you need a telephone. Third, you need a device, called a modem, to connect the two. To go on-line means to connect your computer to other computers over telephone lines.

You have only to dial a phone number and you are all set to go. Today there are many services you can link up with. The information available from them is stored on disks and is called a data base. You have to pay to use some of the information, but there are also hundreds of free sources, as well as free electronic bulletin boards and message-exchange centers where you can link up with an electronic "pen pal."

Two of the most popular data bases for home computer users are The Source and CompuServe. Both of these offer many services. You can get news, weather, and all kinds of other information. You can play games by yourself or with others, shop, place ads, or "chat." "Chat" lets you talk to anyone

who happens to be on-line at that time. You "talk" by typing out messages on your keyboard and reading on your monitor screen what others type out in reply. There is never a time when you don't have someone to talk to if you are on-line with the world.

Use Insect Spray to Debug a Computer

NONSENSE

You should certainly never spray insecticide on your computer! In computer talk, a bug is an error in a program that prevents the program from working properly. Correcting the error is called debugging. You shouldn't kick your computer either, but you can boot it. To boot a computer means to start it or restart it by loading its operating system into its temporary memory. "Bug" and "boot" are only two of the well-known English words that have special meanings in computer language.

Here are some others. "Software" doesn't mean objects that are cottony and soft to the touch. "Software" means computer programs or imput data such as those stored on cartridges, tapes, and disks. On the other hand, "hardware" refers to the physical parts of a computer system, such as the keyboard, the monitor screen, the CPU, and memory chips.

A "floppy," or a "floppy disk," in computer

talk is a plastic disk that is used to store information for a computer on its magnetic surface. It's called a floppy because it is thin and flexible. Most home and personal computers use floppies that are five and one-quarter inches in diameter and held in a stiff cardboard sleeve.

Here are some other computer words whose meanings are different from what you might expect: "bit," "byte," and "peripherals." Do you know any of them?

All Computer Printers Work
Like Typewriters

NONSENSE

There are at least four different kinds of printers that can be attached to a computer, and only one of these works like a typewriter. This kind is usually called a letter-quality printer because its print is just like that of a letter you type on a typewriter. As with a typewriter, this kind of printer uses individual "dies" or impressions of each character. These are mounted on a small plastic or metal wheel, thimble, or ball. In printing, the wheel or ball spins around so that the right character hits an inked ribbon, leaving an impression on the paper.

The least expensive kind of computer printer is called a thermal (heat) printer. Thermal printers work by burning patterns of dots onto special heat-sensitive paper. They are fairly fast and very quiet, but the special paper is expensive and thermal printers can be awkward to use.

Dot-matrix printers also use patterns of dots to produce printed characters, but they do this on regular paper. They are very fast and fairly inexpensive. They can also be used to produce graphics—pictures of all kinds. They do all this by means of a print head that holds a set of tiny wire pins. The pins are driven against the paper through an inked ribbon. Dot-formed characters are the ones we usually associate with computers.

Ink-jet printers are less common than the other kinds. In these, a little nozzle squirts a measured jet of ink onto the paper to form characters. Ink-jet printers are very quiet and produce very good quality print.

Computer Games Are Nothing
but Shoot-'em-ups

NONSENSE

Computer games are not just shoot-'em-ups like most of those you find in the video arcades. Some of the most popular home computer games are called adventure games. Imagine yourself as the hero or heroine in an adventure story, or in a science-fiction story,

or in a mystery. Imagine yourself being faced with making choices at every stage. And each choice that you make changes the things that happen to your character. That's what adventure games are like. Adventure-game players need fast minds, not fast fingers, to play the game well.

An adventure game puts you in a strange place or in a strange predicament. It assigns you some task: find the treasure, rescue a prince or princess, solve the mystery. To win the game you have to figure out what to do and how to do it. You input your instructions, using a keyboard, by typing either a few words, such as "WALK NORTH" or "OPEN DOOR," or certain letter commands that stand for whole words. A complex adventure game may take you hours to play (but usually not at one sitting).

Some computer adventure games are all text. Others combine text and pictures on the screen. In many games, the character you play changes as the game goes on. You gain strength or experience or some valuable skill. You also have to choose among a variety of weapons or tools or some other commodity, or among a variety of routes. One choice may help you, while another may prove your undoing.

Adventure games are enjoyable even if you don't win. Here is a very simple adventure game. It offers you one choice. The right one leads to a treasure, the wrong one to something terrible. The program is written in **BASIC** and will run on most home computers:

```
10 PRINT "YOU ARE STANDING BEFORE"
11 PRINT " TWO CLOSED DOORS."
20 PRINT "A HUNGRY TIGER WAITS BEHIND ONE
   DOOR."
30 PRINT "A VAST TREASURE OF COMPUTER"
31 PRINT "GAMES IS BEHIND THE OTHER."
40 PRINT "DO YOU OPEN THE DOOR ON THE RIGHT"
41 PRINT "OR THE LEFT?"
42 PRINT "TYPE THE WORD 'RIGHT' OR 'LEFT' AND"
43 PRINT "PRESS RETURN."
50 INPUT A$
60 IF A$="RIGHT" GOTO 80
70 IF A$="LEFT" GOTO 90
75 IF A$< >"RIGHT" GOTO 40: IF A$< >"LEFT"
   GOTO 40
```

```
80 PRINT "CONGRATULATIONS! YOU HAVE WON"
81 PRINT "THE COMPUTER GAMES.": END
90 PRINT "GRRR…": END
```

Computers Can Help
Doctors Diagnose Illnesses

Computers are already helping doctors to diagnose very particular kinds of illnesses. For example, a program named MYCIN diagnoses a disease called meningitis. Another program called PUFF diagnoses lung diseases. Still another program called ONCOCIN selects the best treatments for cancer patients. All of these programs are called expert systems.

An expert system is a computer program that tries to copy exactly the methods used by a human expert in a particular field of knowledge. The system allows someone who is not an expert on meningitis, for example, to diagnose and treat the disease almost as accurately as an expert in the field.

You may ask if an expert system works *almost* as accurately, why bother using it? Why not just call on the expert? The answer is that human experts are not always available. They may be thousands of miles away. But an expert system is always available. It's as close as the nearest phone that ties into a computer.

Expert systems are used in areas other than medicine—in weather prediction, for example, in engineering, and even in computer design. In fact, new computer programs are so complex and take so much time to write that human designers almost always have to have expert system help. At present, expert systems can run only on the larger, high-speed computers.

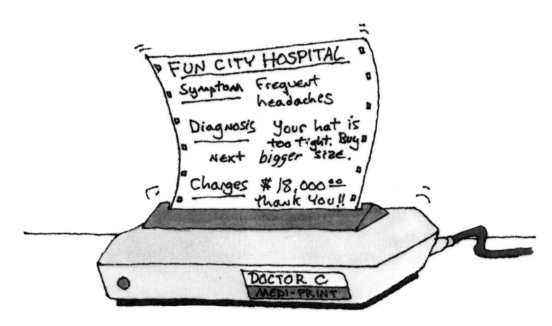

Computers Always Beat
Human Chess Players

NONSENSE

Some of the new home chess computers play very good chess. They can beat most average players. They never make obvious mistakes such as leaving their pieces where they can be taken on the next move. But no chess computers are better than the world's best chess players—the International Grand Masters.

Computers and people play chess very differently. Computers are programmed to assign values to pieces and to positions on the board. The program includes instructions about the rules of chess—how each piece may move on the board, for example. There are also instructions for a number of different opening moves.

Once a game is under way, a computer goes through every possible move it can make and every possible reply from the opponent. Then it selects what it sees as the best move. Computers are very fast. But the number of possible moves in chess is enormous, so the search can take a long time. Even superfast computers can look ahead at only a limited number of moves in a reasonable time.

People play chess in a different way. It seems that good players through much practice view chess pieces in patterns rather than as individual units. They don't consider every possible move of every piece on the board before making a decision. This saves them a lot of time and effort. Learning to play chess well is like learning to read well. A good reader will read in phrases, and will often skim sentences. Similarly, a good chess player sees familiar patterns on the chess board. Then the player makes a careful decision on his or her next move.

A Mouse Is Sometimes Used
with a Computer

SENSE

The mouse that is used with computers is not a brown, furry rodent that likes cheese. A computer mouse is a small device about as big as your palm. It has small wheels or a ball on the bottom and can roll freely on a desk. As you move the mouse around, the wheels move and the movement is coded and electrically sent by cable to the computer.

On the monitor screen, the movement of the mouse appears as a blinking dot of light called a cursor. If you move the mouse to the left of the desk, the cursor moves to the left, and so on.

Computer mice can be used as pointers. Suppose a list of programs appears on the screen. You can roll the mouse around until the cursor is over the program you want. Then you press a button on the mouse and that lets the computer know what you want it to do.

Still another way to use a mouse is in making computer drawings called graphics. Graphics can be charts, graphs, or even computer art. A mouse is really best used with a word-processing program. The mouse provides a fast way of pointing to a particular word or sentence that you want to change. More programs and more ways of using mice are just now being developed. Perhaps by the time you read this your home computer will have its own friendly mouse.

Computers Are Good for Controlling Home Appliances

NONSENSE

Home computers can be used to control appliances such as television sets or lamps, but there are much easier and better ways to control such things. Newspaper and magazine articles often describe how a home computer can be used to adjust the temperature of the house, or to turn on the coffeepot before you get up in the morning—to do automatically all sorts of things to make your life easier.

Computers *can* be programmed to do these things and more. They can turn the furnace on and off, adjust the humidifier and turn on an oven to bake a cake. Home computers can do all these things, but why bother? A simple thermostat will control the temperature in the house. And a five-dollar timer can turn on a lamp or a coffeepot just as well as a five-hundred-dollar computer.

Of course many appliances have built-in

computers or micro-processors, so-called dedicated computers. For example, microwave ovens often have computers that control their operation. The computer in tne oven is dedicated to one job, controlling the oven. This kind of dedicated computer probably cost the manufacturer only a few dollars. Dedicated computers can be found in automobiles, where they are used to check the operation of the engine, in "smart" house thermostats, in television sets, radios, and in many high fidelity components.

There is not much sense, though, in using home computers to do the jobs that can easily be done with other, cheaper automatic devices.

Computers May Work Better on Rainy Days

SENSE

The reason that computers may work better on rainy days than on dry days has to do with static electricity. The spark that jumps from your finger when you walk across a carpeted floor is caused by static electricity. Static electricity is much more likely to be produced on a dry day than on a rainy day. That tiny spark of static electricity may startle you but it is harmless—except to a computer. The spark may cause a computer to make an error or even lose some of its stored memory.

Whenever any electricity flows, even sparks of static electricity, electro-magnetic waves are generated that can cause interference with a computer. EMI (Electro-Magnetic Interference) can be just a minor nuisance or it can be a major concern. With a home computer, you may just have to restart the program if EMI causes a problem. But think of what could happen if electro-magnetic waves interfered with a spacecraft's computer or a large computer that the government uses to store tax returns? Those problems may not be so simple to fix.

Meanwhile, there are several things you can do at home to guard against computer failure from static electricity. If your computer room is carpeted, you may be having problems with static electricity during wintertime when the air in a room is very dry. Try spraying the carpet with a light mixture of fabric softener and water to get rid of the static electricity. You can also use a humidifier to make the air as moist as it would be on a rainy day.

Baseball Players Can Be
Chosen by Computers

SENSE

Imagine that you're the manager of a major league baseball team. It's two out in the ninth inning of the last game of the World Series. Bases are loaded, and your team is two runs behind. The pitcher is up next, but you're sending in a pinch hitter. You walk over to the computer in the dugout and punch a few keys. The computer comes up with the name of the player you should send to the plate. You decide the computer knows best and tell that player to go to bat.

Does this sound like science fiction? Well, it isn't. Some major league teams are already using computers to help them make decisions like this. One of the programs they are using is named **EDGE**.

EDGE was written by a baseball fan and an amateur computer programmer. In order for **EDGE** to work, all kinds of data must be collected, including the names of the batter

and pitcher, what happens with each pitch of the game—did the pitcher pitch a strike or the batter get a base hit?—and what kind of surface the game was played on. The team statistician—the person who records hits, errors, etc.—is the one who usually collects this information. Then the information is inputted into the computer.

Two of the teams that have used **EDGE** are the Chicago White Sox and the Oakland Athletics. The program showed that the Chicago hitters were hitting many long fly balls that were just short of the stands. So management moved home plate closer to the stands and increased the number of team home runs!

Oakland used the program to help decide what batting order to adopt against particular pitchers on different teams. Of course, the computer doesn't ensure that your team will win. The year the New York Yankees began to use this program was a year they didn't win in their division.

Use Common Sense to
Take Care of a Home Computer

SENSE

Taking care of a home computer is not much different from taking care of a television set or a high-fidelity system. A computer has two kinds of parts: electrical and mechanical. The electrical parts you should have little to do with. If something happens to any of them, it will have to be replaced in a repair shop. The mechanical parts have to be kept clean to work properly.

Here are some commonsense hints about what to do to keep your home computer operating trouble-free. Disk drives or cassette recorders need to be kept clean and dust-free. It's a good idea to keep them covered when not in use. You can buy kits that clean their inner workings. These are easy to use. Follow the directions on the package.

Computer disks, cassettes, and cartridges should be stored in their jackets like records and music tapes. Keep them away from dust,

heat, and water. Also, keep them away from magnetic fields such as are given off by a television set or any electrical appliance. Never bend a disk or touch its surface, or touch the surface of a cassette tape.

A monitor or a television set should be dusted and its screen should be cleared once in a while. Keyboards should be covered when not in use to prevent dust from getting inside. Keys don't have to be hit hard to work—and they will last much longer if you have a soft touch. Printers should be covered when not in use. You may have to change the print head and the ribbon from time to time. Follow the directions in the manual or ask a dealer how to do it.

Keep connecting cables out of the way of pets or people. Tripping over a cable can hurt not only the computer, it can hurt you as well. Keep a diagram of which cable is connected to which plug. This will help you if the cables are accidentally pulled out or you move the computer. Taking proper care of your computer is just a matter of common sense.

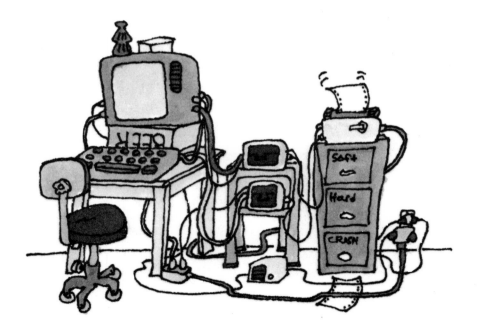

Shopping for a Home Computer Is Easy

NONSENSE

Shopping for a home computer the first time is different from shopping for most other things. Many first-time buyers are not sure what kind of computer they want, what is available, or even why they want a computer. And a lot of the salespeople now selling low-price computers, costing several hundred dollars or less, know little more than the customers. Higher-priced computers are usually sold in computer specialty shops. Salespeople there generally have more knowledge of the computers they are selling.

Here are some things you can do to make computer shopping easier. First, ask plenty of questions of your friends who have computers. Ask them what problems they have had and what they would suggest you do to avoid the problems. Ask different people the same question. Don't be afraid of appearing

54

stupid. Keep asking questions until you understand the answers.

Second, figure out who in your family will use the computer and for what reasons. Find out if the computer you have in mind will actually do what you want it to do. That means find out what software (variety of programs) is available for the computer. The best computers in the world are of no use without programs that meet your needs.

Be sure you know what peripherals (hardware accessories) you will need. You will need either a cassette recorder or a disk drive to load programs into. You will need a monitor or a TV to show you what you have inputted as you go along. If you want to make copies of your work, you will need a printer. These can cost more than the computer itself. You can buy computers that come in a package with some or all of these peripherals. Before you go shopping, read books and magazines about computers or ask your friends to find out what's currently available.

Finally, take your time when you shop. A computer from a discount store may cost you less, but you may not get the service you would from a store that sells only computers. Decide what's most important for you. There are many good, inexpensive computers currently available. There may be better computers coming along in the future, but the one you buy now will keep you entertained and informed for many years.

About the Author

Seymour Simon was born in New York City. He received his B.A. degree from City College, New York, and did graduate work there. He was a science teacher for a number of years and is now writing and editing full time.

Mr. Simon is the author of dozens of highly acclaimed science books for young readers, including *Killer Whales*; *How to Be a Space Scientist in Your Own Home*; *Body Sense, Body Nonsense*; and *The Dinosaur is the Biggest Animal That Ever Lived and Other Wrong Ideas You Thought Were True*. More than thirty of his books have been selected as Outstanding Science Trade Books for Children by the National Science Teachers Association. He lives with his wife and two sons in Great Neck, New York.

About the Artist

Steven Lindblom received his B.F.A. in illustration from the Rhode Island School of Design. He is now a full-time writer and illustrator. He and his author-illustrator wife, True Kelley, live in Warner, New Hampshire, with their daughter, Jada, in a house Mr. Lindblom designed and built himself.